Human Rights in Focus: Refugees

Michael V. Uschan

San Diego, CA

© 2018 ReferencePoint Press, Inc.
Printed in the United States

For more information, contact:
ReferencePoint Press, Inc.
PO Box 27779
San Diego, CA 92198
www. ReferencePointPress.com

LIBRARY OF CONGRESS CATALOGING-IN-PUBLICATION DATA

Name: Uschan, Michael V., 1948- author.
Title: Human Rights in Focus: Refugees/by Michael V. Uschan.
Description: San Diego, CA : Reference Press, Inc., 2017. | Series: Human
  Rights in Focus | Includes bibliographical references and index.
Identifiers: LCCN 2016055059 (print) | LCCN 2016057615 (ebook) | ISBN
  9781682822333 (hardback) | ISBN 9781682822340 (eBook)
Subjects: LCSH: Refugees--Juvenile literature.
Classification: LCC JV6346.R4 U73 2017 (print) | LCC JV6346.R4 (ebook) | DDC
  323.6/31--dc23
LC record available at https://lccn.loc.gov/2016055059

Contents

Seeking New Lives

A crowd of more than seventy-five thousand people cheered as athletes participating in the 2016 Summer Olympics marched into Maracanã Stadium in Rio de Janeiro, Brazil, on August 5. All of the 205 nations competing in the Olympics received loud and warm receptions. But the crowd also gave a hearty welcome to the first-ever Refugee Olympic Team, made up of ten athletes who had no nation to represent. The athletes—five from South Sudan, two from Syria, two from the Democratic Republic of the Congo, and one from Ethiopia—were invited to compete under the Olympic flag to raise awareness of the global refugee crisis.

One of the refugee athletes was Yiech Pur Biel, who was ten years old when he fled Sudan to escape civil war in 2005. After spending a decade in a refugee camp in Kenya, Biel was picked for the Refugee Olympic Team. At the Olympics, he competed in the 800-meter run. Biel did not win a medal—but that was never his goal. "I have a mission to tell the world we refugees are human beings like other people," Biel says. "And if you give us a chance to participate in anything we can prove that to be called a refugee is only a name."[1]

Some refugees are people who flee their native countries to escape war. Others leave because they are persecuted or fear being persecuted for their race, religion, nationality, or political views. Biel and the other nine members of the Refugee Olympic Team were among tens of millions of people who have left their homelands for those reasons. In 2016 the United Nations (UN) reported that there were at least 21.3 million refugees, half of them younger than eighteen.

Refugees and Human Rights

Refugees leave behind their homes, family and friends, and most (if not all) of their possessions. They flee because of discrimination due to their race or religion or because their human rights are threatened. Rights under threat commonly include equal treatment under the law, freedom of expression, the right to work, and social rights such as access to education and medical care. The fact that they are seeking safety makes refugees different from immigrants, who choose to leave their home in search of a better life.

Although most nations grant basic rights to their citizens, some do not. In fact, many people become refugees because their nations deny them such rights. However, once people become refugees it is hard for them to regain those rights, because they lack status as citizens of any nation. Without rights to protect them, refugees often find themselves facing a seemingly endless round of hardships.

The right to travel and live where one wants is a basic human right, and when refugees leave their homelands they must move and live somewhere else. However, governments sometimes refuse to let refugees enter their country. In 2015 Germany and several other nations admitted tens of thousands of refugees from Africa and the Middle East. But several nations—including Greece, Bulgaria, Macedonia, Turkey, and Hungary—put up physical barriers and used armed police and soldiers to block refugees from entering. Unable to return home or move elsewhere, hundreds of thousands of people were herded into refugee camps funded and operated by various countries, the UN, and charitable groups. Here they typically stay until those entities decide what to do with them.

Many camps fail to provide refugees with adequate shelter, food, education, security, and medical care. For example, in 2016, Hendiya Asseni, a sixty-two-year-old Syrian refugee, was housed in a refugee camp in northern Greece that was a former toilet paper factory. Asseni angrily complained about his living conditions: "It's insulting. But then everything here is insulting—the life, the food, the fact we have a toilet in front of our tent."[2] In addition to being cramped and dirty and lacking adequate facilities, such camps are often unsafe; workers and soldiers charged with guarding refugees sometimes physically or sexually abuse them, even children.

Asseni and other refugees had no control over what was happening to them because they had no government to protect their rights. In Africa, where people have been fleeing civil war and various forms of persecution for a long time, refugees like Biel have been forced to live in camps for years because no nation will accept them. Some refugees pay criminals to smuggle them into European countries, where they hope to seek asylum, or the right to live in those nations. But criminals often rob refugees or transport them to areas where they still are unable to enter countries where they would be safe.

Refugees Need Help

The UN plays a major role in helping refugees around the world. It primarily does so through its office of the United Nations High

Commissioner for Refugees (UNHCR). When the UNHCR was established in 1950, there were only about 1 million refugees worldwide. Today there are close to 22 million. Sadako Ogata of Japan headed the UNHCR from 1991 to 2000. In a 1993 report, Ogata claimed that the most serious problem facing refugees was the loss of their human rights. Because of that, she said, "the refugee issue must be put to all governments and peoples as a test of their commitment to human rights."[3] Her declaration was as true then as it is in the twenty-first century.

Chapter 1

A Global Problem

In 2017 the world was struggling to cope with the worst refugee crisis since World War II, when fighting devastated Europe and forced 60 million people to flee their homes. The UN Refugee Agency reported that by the end of 2015, 21.3 million people had become refugees, either because of war or because they feared being (or were being) persecuted for their race, religion, nationality, or political views. The figure was released on June 20, a day that since 2001 the UN has designated as World Refugee Day to focus attention on the plight of refugees.

One of the cruelest aspects of the crisis is that boys and girls younger than eighteen make up nearly half the global refugee population. That means that in 2015, nearly one in every two hundred children in the world was a refugee. Many young refugees flee with parents who are trying to keep their children alive or family members who are trying to give them a chance at a better life elsewhere. Other children flee on their own when their parents are killed. Some have families that arrange for them to flee by themselves, leaving behind older relatives.

It is hard to overstate just how drastically refugees' lives change because of this decision. Refugees abandon nearly everything, including family, friends, and most of their possessions. This is hard for most people to bear, but it is especially difficult for young people. When twelve-year-old Mohammed and his family fled fighting in Aleppo, Syria, in 2015, he said, "I'll miss my school and my friends so much."[4] Gulwali Passarlay was twelve when he left Afghanistan with his brother after his family was killed in an ongoing war. Passarlay also fled because he

> "I had a beautiful life. I was a shepherd [but] unfortunately events happened [and we] had to flee for our lives."[5]
>
> —Gulwali Passarlay, who left Afghanistan when he was twelve

feared he would be forced to become a soldier for the Taliban, an extremist group fighting for control of Afghanistan. "I had a beautiful life," he says. "I was a shepherd [but] unfortunately events happened [and we] had to flee for our lives."[5]

The Current State of the Crisis

Passarlay and other refugees are just one part of a greater global crisis. Tens of millions more have left their homes for similar reasons, but not all of them are classified as refugees. In 2015 the UN considered 65.3 million people to be *displaced* as a result of persecution, conflict, generalized violence, or human rights violations. Just 21.3 million of these were considered to be refugees, however. Since 1951 the UN has defined refugees specifically as people who, due to danger from war or a "well-founded fear of being persecuted for reasons of race, religion, nationality, membership of a particular

Children and women wait in line for food at a makeshift refugee camp in Greece. Children make up nearly half of the global refugee population.

social group or political opinion,"[6] have fled their country and cannot return. The other 40.8 million people are not considered refugees but rather displaced. These are people who have fled their homes for similar reasons as refugees but still reside within their native countries (development organizations like the World Bank often refer to them as "internally displaced people").

In 2015 the vast majority of refugees (54 percent) were from just three nations—Somalia (1.1 million), Afghanistan (2.7 million), and Syria (4.9 million). Refugees' other countries of origin include Iraq, Libya, Eritrea, the Democratic Republic of the Congo, Sudan, Yemen, Nigeria, Iran, Pakistan, and Bangladesh. Many refugees try to get to European nations including Germany, France, Italy, and the United Kingdom because of their peaceful interiors and the fact that they guarantee their citizens basic human rights. Refugees from Cuba, South America, and Mexico often try to enter the United States.

Experts have predicted the refugee crisis will get worse, because the problems that caused it show no signs of stopping. One such expert is David Miliband, a former foreign minister from Great Britain who in 2016 headed the International Rescue Committee, which aids refugees and others who need help. "This [crisis] is not a blip," warned Miliband in 2016. "The forces that are driving more and more people from their homes—weak states, big tumults within the Islamic world, a divided international system. . . . None of these things are likely to abate soon."[7]

Two Historic Refugee Crises

There are many reasons people become refugees, but loss and destruction from war is the most common. Besides being the two largest refugee crises in the past eight decades, the refugee catastrophes of World War II and 2016 have something else in common: They were both born as a result of military invasions that began wars. Both invasions unleashed unintended political and social consequences that devastated their respective geographical areas long after the initial fighting ended.

Germany started World War II on September 1, 1939, when it invaded Poland. Over the next few years it conquered most of Europe. The war in Europe ended on May 7, 1945, when Germany surrendered to the Allies, a group of nations that included

East German refugees make their way to Berlin in 1945. The refugee population following the end of World War II continued to grow as people fled communism.

the United States and the Union of Soviet Socialist Republics, or USSR (which included modern-day Russia). One unexpected consequence of Germany's initial invasion was that after the war, a large part of Europe became Communist. This was because the USSR, a Communist country, took control of the nations it had freed from German rule, such as Poland, Romania, and Hungary (it also retained part of Germany, which became East Germany). Even after the fighting stopped, Europe's refugee population continued to grow, as millions of people fled their homes to avoid living under communism. The UN estimated that in 1951, six years after the war ended, the spread of communism had generated 15 million European refugees from Soviet rule, including at least 12 million ethnic Germans.

The modern refugee crisis is centered in the Middle East. It can similarly be said to have its roots in an invasion—the US invasion of Iraq on March 20, 2003. President George W. Bush's goal was to remove then president Saddam Hussein from power. Bush argued that Hussein had sheltered terrorists connected with the September 11, 2001, terrorist attacks that killed nearly three thousand Americans. Bush also claimed that Iraq posed a danger to other countries because it had weapons of mass destruction, a claim that was never proven.

The United States invaded Iraq despite the concerns of many US and world leaders, who worried that ousting Saddam Hussein could create more problems. In October 2002, six months before the invasion, even longtime Libyan dictator Muammar Gaddafi warned, "Iraq could end up becoming the staging ground for [the terrorist group] Al-Qaeda, because if the Saddam government collapses, it will be anarchy in Iraq."[8]

Gaddafi's prediction was correct. The invasion unleashed numerous political and religious forces that spread fighting, instability, and disorder to other Middle Eastern countries, including Gaddafi's own. All of these events helped create a historic flood of refugees.

South American Refugees

Because of their large numbers, refugees from the Middle East have gotten most of the world's attention in recent years. But large numbers of refugees from Mexico, South America, and Central American countries such as Honduras, El Salvador, Costa Rica, Belize, Panama, and Guatemala have also fled their lands due to violence from criminal organizations, gangs, and drug cartels. In 2016 Adrian Edwards, a spokesperson for the UNHCR, commented on the dangers those refugees faced: "We are particularly concerned about the rising numbers of unaccompanied children and women on the run who face forced recruitment into criminal gangs, sexual- and gender-based violence and murder."

El Salvador is considered to be especially dangerous because it has the highest homicide rate in the world. In 2015 there were 104.2 murders for every 100,000 Salvadorans. For comparison, there are 4.5 murders per 100,000 people who live in the United States. The UNHCR is trying to allocate more resources to care for the increasing number of refugees from that area and working with other countries in the region—such as Mexico and the United States—to help them.

Nora Sturm, "UNHCR Calls for Urgent Action as Central America Asylum Claims Soar," United Nations High Commissioner for Refugees, April 5, 2016. www.unhcr.org.

The Invasion Incites Chaos and Violence

The invasion of Iraq ended Saddam Hussein's twenty-four-year dictatorship, and US forces captured Baghdad, Iraq's capital, on April 9, 2003. But in a few weeks, rebels known as insurgents began using guerrilla tactics to attack US soldiers. The insurgents soon earned sympathy from millions of Muslims around the world, who were enraged that a Christian nation had invaded a Muslim one. Muslims from many parts of the world traveled to Iraq to defend it, and Islam, from the United States. They continued to attack US and Iraqi forces even after a new Iraqi government was formed. Fighting there has continued on and off ever since.

These events also fueled the refugee crisis. Saddam Hussein was a brutal dictator whose rule routinely violated the rights of Iraqi citizens. Anyone who challenged Saddam Hussein or his policies was beaten, imprisoned, or even killed. However, his iron rule kept in check religious, political, and social forces that could have caused unrest and violence. In Iraq members of the two main sects of Islam—Sunnis and Shias—were often at odds over centuries-old disagreements about religious and social issues. Saddam Hussein's brutal rule clamped down on these disagreements. It also quieted Iraqis who wanted a different type of government. Some Iraqis wanted to form a democracy in which they could freely elect their leaders and enjoy their basic human rights. But others, mostly Sunni Muslims, wanted a government based on religion, specifically laws drawn from the Koran, the Muslim holy book, and other religious teachings. All this dissent simmered under Iraq's tightly controlled surface. Commentator David Francis explains that the one positive aspect of Saddam Hussein's dictatorship was that "his heavy hand was able to keep the country under control [and] under his rule, Iraq was relatively peaceful."[9]

However, Saddam Hussein's fall allowed those various groups to begin fighting about their myriad disagreements. In the next few years, similar struggles over opposing social, religious, and political views spread to neighboring Middle Eastern countries and even other parts of the world. Many of these movements were part of what became known as the Arab Spring, and most were aimed at ending dictatorial regimes similar to that of Saddam Hussein and initiating democratic governments.

By 2015 all-out civil wars or disorder raged in nine nations, including Iraq, Syria, Afghanistan, Nigeria, Sudan, Somalia, and Pakistan. One effect was the overthrow of several dictators, including Gaddafi, who was killed by rebels on October 20, 2011, after forty-two years in power. The resulting violence in those nations forced millions of people to become refugees.

War and Persecution Create Refugees

The flood of refugees has been the greatest and most tragic in Syria, where a civil war began in March 2011. Like citizens of other nations caught up in the Arab Spring, in 2010 Syrians began to protest the dictatorship of President Bashar al-Assad, who had brutally ruled Syria since 2000. The protests began after teenagers who had painted slogans opposing al-Assad were arrested and tortured. The protests gradually developed into a horrific war. By 2016 the conflict had killed an estimated four hundred thousand people. It also displaced half of Syria's population—nearly 11 million people—from their homes. Nearly 5 million of them left Syria.

In addition to being deadly, the fighting that destroyed much of Syria was confusing because so many groups were involved. The Syrian Army was fighting to keep al-Assad in power, and it was aided by Russia. Various rebel groups trying to overthrow al-Assad included prodemocracy factions (helped by the United States) but also Muslim terrorist organizations, like the Islamic State of Iraq and the Levant (ISIS). Mariam Akash, a mother of nine whose husband was killed in the fighting, still lived in Syria in 2014. She vividly explained why so many people had left: "We're just living on the edge of life. We're always nervous, we're always afraid. When there are clashes I keep the children hiding and tell them to, 'Keep your heads down,' I'm always worried about them getting caught in the fighting."[10]

> "We're just living on the edge of life. We're always nervous, we're always afraid."[10]
>
> —Mariam Akash, a mother of nine who lives in Syria

Millions of people have also fled other countries because of religious persecution and civil war. For example, Yiech Pur Biel fled South Sudan in 2005 at age ten to escape civil war and ethnic prejudice. Biel belonged to the Nuor tribe, which has historically clashed with another tribe known as the Dinka. "In Juba (South Sudan), they will kill me," he said, of why he could never go home. "They will know I am Nuor in a moment. Even if you don't have the gar [Nuor tribal scarring], they know. They ask you to open your mouth and speak Dinka, and if you can't, they kill you."[11]

Christians in the Middle East also became endangered. Some dictators, like Saddam Hussein, had historically allowed Christians to live in peace; however, terrorist groups like ISIS threatened to kill non-Muslims who refused to embrace Islam. Some Middle Eastern Christians were killed, but more fled. By 2016 the number of Christians in Iraq, for example, had fallen from 1.5 million in 2003 to fewer than 500,000. Christians in other Muslim

Christianity has come under attack in the Middle East, causing many people to flee their homeland. The number of Christians in Iraq (pictured are people attending a Christian Mass in the Iraqi village of Bartella) has fallen from 1.5 million in 2003 to fewer than 500,000 in 2016.

countries, as well as people of other faiths, also came under attack. This further swelled the flood of refugees.

More Help Is Needed

Many nations have accepted some refugees as citizens or offered them aid until they can find new homes. However, as of 2017, millions were still suffering a stateless existence, trapped between homes they had left and homes they had not yet attained. On September 20, 2016, at a UN summit on the refugee crisis, President Barack Obama described the refugee crisis as one of "epic proportions," saying, "this crisis is a test of our common humanity."[12] Obama said the world needed to show compassion for refugees because "most of them [are] women and children [who] are often fleeing war and terrorism. They're victims."[13]

> "This crisis is a test of our common humanity."[12]
>
> —Barack Obama, forty-fourth US president, addressing the 2016 UN summit on refugees

At the summit, more than fifty nations and organizations pledged $4.5 billion to help refugees (the United States pledged $1 billion). The new aid was badly needed—according to the UN, in 2015 only 81,000 of 960,000 refugees it cared for had been resettled in other countries. The rest were housed in refugee camps that often failed to provide adequate housing, food, and security. Many others were still traveling in the hopes of reaching a country that would accept them.

Despite these pledges, many nations, even wealthy ones, have done little to help refugees. In 2015 Japan accepted only nineteen refugees. Brazil accepted six, and Russia none. Some nations have actively turned against refugees. For example, in 2015 Hungary built a barrier on its border and fired tear gas and water cannons at refugees trying to cross. Meanwhile, Pakistan and Iran have been accused of forcing refugees to go back to their homeland, even though doing so is against international law.

Some nations do not want to accept refugees for cultural reasons. Many refugees—especially those from Syria, Somalia, and Afghanistan—are Muslim. Islamophobia—fear of or discrimination against Muslims—is rampant in certain countries. Muslims follow a certain diet and dress in ways that mainstream populations in some countries, such as the United States, France, and

Protecting the Rights of Stateless People

The UNHCR, also known as the UN Refugee Agency, was created in 1950, five years after the end of World War II. Its initial purpose was to help millions of Europeans who had fled or lost their homes. Today the UNHCR's main mission is to help and protect refugees. One way it does so is to make sure that refugees, who do not belong to any nation, continue to have their human rights protected. "Governments normally guarantee the basic human rights and physical security of citizens," explains the UNHCR. "But when civilians become refugees this safety net disappears." Thus, the UNHCR works to make sure "states are aware of, and act on, their obligations to protect refugees and persons seeking asylum."

One of the most important safeguards the UNHCR provides is to keep refugees from being physically harmed. The agency also provides housing, food, and medical care. It also runs education programs for refugees, teaching them skills they need to adapt to a new country, speak a new language, and be prepared for new jobs.

United Nations High Commissioner for Refugees, "Protecting Refugees: Questions and Answers," February 2, 2002. www.unhcr.org.

Germany, find strange or even offensive. Others worry that Muslim refugees pose a security threat, arguing that ISIS terrorists will pretend to be refugees, enter a country, and stage an attack. Indeed, there have been several terrorist attacks in Europe and the United States that were perpetrated by those loyal to ISIS and connected to countries that produce a lot of refugees. The worst of these occurred in November 2015 in the French cities of Paris and Saint-Denis, when armed terrorists loyal to ISIS attacked in France after having posed as refugees. They killed 130 people in a series of shootings and suicide bombings.

Some nations are also reluctant to accept refugees because they believe the cost of caring for them is too great. For example, in 2016 alone, Germany spent an estimated $2.5 billion just on providing education to the nearly 1 million refugees it accepted. Some Germans worried that schools would be so overwhelmed, they would not be able to educate native-born German students. Germany also faced the expense of providing housing, medical care, and other services for refugees.

It is true that caring for refugees takes a lot of money, good security, and some generosity. But Kenneth Roth, executive director of Human Rights Watch, thinks the high price is worth it. In his opinion, many nations—including very wealthy ones—are not doing what they can to help those most in need of assistance. He even argues that such nations have violated refugees' human rights by not allowing them entrance, failing to make refugee camps give them adequate food and housing, and not allowing them to work. Josephine Liebl of Oxfam's Global Displacement Campaign agrees. Her group is dedicated to helping refugees, and Liebl thinks that too many rich nations talk about helping refugees but do little. "Sympathy about this global crisis will be voiced [by many], but words need action,"[14] she says.

Chapter 2

Why People Become Refugees

Focus Questions

1. Refugees flee their homes because they fear being killed during armed conflict or persecuted because of their race, religion, sexuality, ethnicity, or political beliefs. What situation would be bad enough to force you to become a refugee?

2. Refugees experience dramatic life changes when they leave their homelands. What would change in your life if you became a refugee? Explain your answer.

3. Becoming a refugee means separating from family and friends, becoming homeless, and learning to live in a new country and culture. What do you think would be the hardest part of being a refugee for you, and why?

The decision to become a refugee is one of the hardest any person will ever have to make—it changes one's life forever. Refugees must leave the comfort and safety of their homes and communities. They become homeless for months or even years. They may never again see the friends and relatives they left behind. Because many refugees must flee quickly, they can take only what they can carry or what will fit into a small car. In very poor or rural areas, refugees might even flee on a wagon pulled by a donkey or horse. They do not know where they will end up or what their lives will be like. They only know their journey will feature hardships and danger. Despite such harsh realities, millions of people become refugees each year. They do so for many reasons that share one commonality: Leaving offers them better odds than staying.

Human Rights Violations

Many refugees flee situations because they are threatened with violence, lack freedom to express their political views, are unable to practice their religion or express their sexuality, or are denied other basic human rights. Malith Chan was fourteen years old when soldiers invaded his village in South Sudan and began killing people. "The soldiers just beat everybody, shooting the children—kids even two years old—killing the old people,"[15] says Chan. He and his younger brother escaped the slaughter and traveled to the Kakuma Refugee Camp in Kenya. They lived there for several years before being moved to Phoenix, Arizona, with the help of a Roman Catholic relief agency.

> "The soldiers just beat everybody, shooting the children—kids even two years old—killing the old people."[15]
>
> —Malith Chan, who fled South Sudan at age fourteen

Clampdowns on freedom of speech also create refugee situations. Mezar Matar was a journalist in Raqqa, Syria, in 2013 when ISIS seized control of his hometown. Matar began to fear for his life after he reported on protests against ISIS. "I received threats from them," says Matar. "I was afraid everyday, when I would walk home, I would fear from the cars that drove by me—I was scared they would abduct me."[16] Matar escaped and went to Turkey, but he hopes to return to Syria someday if ISIS can be defeated.

Selam Gebru fled her home in Eritrea for a different reason—religious persecution. Gebru was Christian in a Muslim country. "[I] was forbidden to worship," says Gebru of her life in Eritrea. "All the churches were closed, all the Christians were being hounded by the government, so all in all I decided to flee home."[17]

Sexual orientation is yet another factor that drives refugees from their homelands. Many Muslim nations discriminate against gay people, who are sometimes imprisoned or killed if their government regards homosexuality as sinful. In September 2016 the Central Okanagan Refugee Committee in Kelowna, British Columbia, welcomed a gay man who had fled this kind of persecution in Syria. "Getting across the border into Iraq gave him space from those who seemed immediately after his hide, but [the Middle East is] not a gay-friendly environment in any way, shape or form,"[18] says Tom Kemp, who chairs the group.

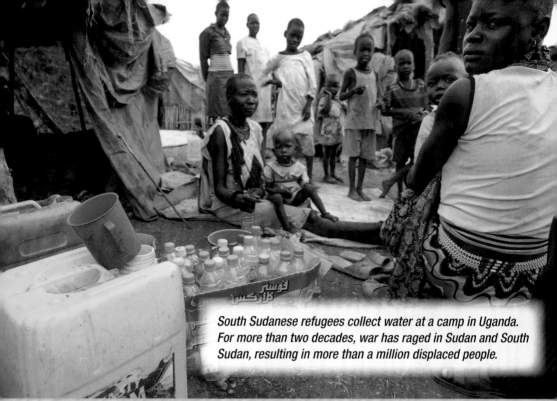

South Sudanese refugees collect water at a camp in Uganda. For more than two decades, war has raged in Sudan and South Sudan, resulting in more than a million displaced people.

War Creates Refugees

However, the vast majority of people become refugees because of war. Indeed, the modern refugee crisis is greater than at any time since World War II, in part because there has been more war globally than at any time since then. In recent years civil wars have been fought in nine Middle Eastern and North African nations—Afghanistan, Iraq, Syria, Yemen, Libya, Somalia, South Sudan, and parts of Turkey and Nigeria. Just as during World War II, the death and destruction of war has forced millions of people to flee for their lives.

War for control of the African nation of Sudan has raged between two tribes—the Dinka and the Nuor—off and on for more than two decades. In 2011 the country split into Sudan and South Sudan, but war continued even after that. On September 16, 2016, the UN Refugee Agency said a new surge in fighting had forced 185,000 people to flee from South Sudan very quickly. Their exodus pushed the number of South Sudanese refugees to more than 1 million.

One of those refugees is Tamma Joyce. When gunshots were fired in the South Sudanese village of Lainya, she and other people began running. Joyce ran home but could not find her parents.

Video of ISIS Life

Many refugees have come from Raqqa, Syria, and a 2016 video made secretly by two women shows why. The video shows armed soldiers of ISIS patrolling nearly deserted streets heavily damaged by fighting. One woman, Oum Mohammad, discusses the barbaric death sentences ISIS imposes for violating rules. "They execute with bullets, desecrate the body, decapitate it, stick the head on a spike and put it on display at the roundabout or they will put the body on the road and force cars to run it over until nothing is left," she says in the video. She also discusses how ISIS has severely limited women's rights and forced them to wear tent-like clothing that completely covers their bodies and faces. Mohammad says she wishes she could "take off the niqab [the face covering] and the darkness that cloaks us." The video shows the women trying to buy some hair dye in a store. Pictures of women on the dye boxes have been colored over, due to a prohibition on showing a woman's face in public. "All women like to show their faces," says Mohammad. "We've lost that option. We've lost our femininity." Mohammad and her friend were able to send the video to a Swedish news station, which posted it online so the world could see the reality of life under ISIS.

Siobhan McFadyen, "Undercover Film Shows Inhuman Existence of Women Living Under ISIS Rule in Raqqa," *Mirror* (London), March 14, 2016. www.mirror.co.uk.

Fearing for her life, she hurriedly filled a backpack with clothes, grabbed her cell phone, and ran away. The nineteen-year-old ended up in a refugee camp in Uganda. She does not know what happened to her parents, but she says, "I keep hoping to see them. I feel very bad. I just hope we are reunited."[19] Somalia, too, has been a battleground since 1991, when the government collapsed. War has been fought to control various parts of that African nation and has featured the Muslim extremist group al Shabab, rival political parties, and foreign soldiers from Kenya.

Arab Spring and Winter

Most of the wars in the Middle East began after the US invasion of Iraq, and specifically after a period known as the Arab Spring. The Arab Spring was born on December 17, 2010, when Mohamed Bouazizi, a street vendor in Ben Arous, Tunisia, set himself on fire to protest his treatment by the government. For years officials had harassed him and seized his merchandise because he could not afford a vendor's license. Bouazizi's death on January 4, 2011, sparked a backlash. People protested in the streets, sometimes violently, against the brutal way in which Tunisia's government routinely treated its citizens and denied their basic human rights. The protests were aimed at protecting these rights and at establishing a more democratic government. The prodemocracy movement was so powerful that it forced President Zine El Abidine Ben Ali to flee to Saudi Arabia and ended his twenty-three-year reign.

Similar uprisings, protests, and riots spread quickly to neighboring Middle Eastern countries also ruled by authoritarian and dictatorial leaders. These resulted in the overthrow of Hosni Mubarak in Egypt, Muammar Gaddafi in Libya, and Ali Abdullah Saleh in Yemen. These were leaders who had routinely and brutally denied citizens basic human rights, such as the right to publicly criticize the government and freedom from unjust imprisonment. Other countries that experienced Arab Spring–related protests or uprisings included Syria, Bahrain, Algeria, Iraq, Jordan, Kuwait, Morocco, Oman, and Saudi Arabia.

However, the prodemocracy tone of the uprisings did not last long. The Arab Spring quickly faded when supporters of authoritarian regimes either fought back or took advantage of the power vacuums created by the chaos. "The peaceful demonstrations that were supposed to bring democracy have instead given way to bloodshed and chaos, with the forces of tyranny trying to turn back the clock," explains Georgetown University Middle East expert Daniel Byman. "It is too soon to say that the Arab Spring is gone, never to resurface. But the Arab Winter has clearly arrived."[20]

In Egypt the attempt to transition to democracy ended in a military coup, mass arrests, and another repressive government. Meanwhile, similar attempts in Libya, Yemen, and Tunisia ignited civil wars. The most devastating civil war by far has been in Syria. The result of the 2011 failure to overthrow President Bashar al-Assad has been continuous, savage fighting that has forced half of Syria's 23 million citizens from their homes and killed four hundred thousand people.

The threat of dying in that terrible conflict caused Hashem al-Souki, his wife, and three sons to flee their small community near Damascus, the capital of Syria. A government worker, al-Souki was arrested and imprisoned for several months in 2012

A masked soldier displays the ISIS banner in the deserts of the Middle East. The extremist group uses brutality and terrorist tactics to seize territory, which has created a flood of refugees.

because he opposed al-Assad's rule. Al-Souki was not alone in this treatment—from 2011 to 2013 at least eleven thousand people were tortured and even killed for opposing al-Assad. Al-Souki made the difficult decision to leave Syria after being freed. When his father asked him why he could not stay, he replied, "Papa, I'm sorry. But it's unbearable here. I have to go—not for me, but for my children and my wife."[21] His family made it to safety in Egypt on June 27, 2013.

The war al-Souki fled was still raging on September 26, 2016, when more than two hundred people were killed in and around Aleppo in just a few days after a weeklong cease-fire expired. "I've never seen so many people dying in one place," said Mohammad Zein Khandaqani, a doctor. "It's terrifying today. In less than one hour the Russian planes have killed more than 50 people and injured more than two hundred."[22] One reason Syria's civil war has lasted so long is that the United States and Russia have indirectly joined the fighting by supporting various groups. The United States has backed Syrian rebels who are trying to overthrow al-Assad, whom Russia supports.

Continuous warfare and antigovernment sentiments have shattered some Middle Eastern nations so much that Muslim extremist groups have been able to win control of parts of them. The most powerful of these groups is ISIS, and the despotic way it rules territory has created a new flood of refugees.

Refugees Flee from War

ISIS began in 1999 as an offshoot of al Qaeda, which was founded in 1988 by Osama bin Laden. It is one of several radical groups that support what is often (and controversially) called Islamic fundamentalism. This extreme outlook is based on Sharia law, which is derived from the Koran, the Muslim holy book, and the Sunna, the teachings of the Prophet Mohammed, who founded Islam in the seventh century. Sharia replaces democratic methods of government with religious rules that strictly control all aspects of life, including daily routine, family and religious obligations, and financial dealings. While most Muslims reject fundamentalism because it ignores basic human rights and is not an accurate interpretation of their religion, extremist groups like ISIS use it to further their cause.

> "It's unbearable here. I have to go—not for me, but for my children and my wife."[21]
>
> —Hashem al-Souki, who left Syria in 2012 because of continuous warfare

Despite its overall unpopularity, ISIS has been able to use terrorist tactics to seize territory from several nations. Busy fighting political unrest and fallout from the Arab Spring, several nations were unable to protect large swaths of their land. In 2014, for example, ISIS took control of large parts of Libya and Iraq and declared the area an Islamic state. Many people soon began to flee because of the harsh new life ISIS imposed on them. "Life under ISIS is not good at all," wrote one man who experienced ISIS's rule in Mosul, Iraq. "Men aren't allowed to cut their beards and they have to shorten their trousers. You shouldn't smoke cigarettes. Women have to wear the niqab [cloth over their face] and cover their hands. In addition they have banned the Internet at home and phone calls."[23] In 2016 a man living in ISIS-controlled Sirte, Libya, told Human Rights Watch, "Everyone is living in fear."[24]

One reason for such fear is the barbaric punishments that ISIS imposes on people who violate its interpretation of Sharia. For example, a groom asked a barber in Fallujah, Iraq, to cut his beard off and shorten his hair so he would look nice for his wedding. Fearing punishment, the barber refused to cut the man's beard but says he "dressed his hair, adding gel to make it look good."[25] The barber was arrested after someone told the local religious authority what he had done. His shop was closed, and he was whipped in public. After receiving fifty of the eighty-lash sentence, the barber fainted and was taken to a hospital.

ISIS soldiers also cut off the hands of those who were convicted of theft. People might also be executed for smoking cigarettes, being gay, listening to Western music, or failing to cooperate with ISIS officials. Christians have been told they will be killed if they do not accept Islam; some refused and have become martyrs (died) for their faith. ISIS death sentences include crucifixion, beheading, and being dismembered with chainsaws, which was the punishment nine young people received in Mosul in 2016 for opposing ISIS. Fundamentalist groups that employ similar tactics include the Taliban, which once controlled most of Afghanistan; Boko Haram in Nigeria; and al Shabab in Somalia. Where these groups have been able to control territory, people have fled for their lives and sought refuge elsewhere in the world.

> "Life under ISIS is not good at all. Men aren't allowed to cut their beards and . . . [women] have to wear the niqab [cloth over their face] and cover their hands. In addition they have banned the Internet at home and phone calls."[23]
>
> —A diary entry of a man who lives under ISIS rule in Mosul, Iraq

Why Women Flee

Many refugees are women. Many leave their homelands, either alone or with their families, for the usual reasons people become refugees—to escape war or various forms of persecution. However, women face unique and brutal challenges because of their gender. Extremist groups like ISIS believe women are inferior to men and must be subservient to them. This is why when ISIS takes control of an area, it promptly reverses many women's rights. Women can no longer go to school and must wear clothing that entirely covers their bodies and faces. Their movement in public is severely restricted; even when shopping or otherwise out in public, they cannot talk to a man unless they are accompanied by a male family member.

Women also flee because they are forced to endure sexual violence. Boko Haram is an extremist group that is active in Nigeria. In 2014 Boko Haram soldiers kidnapped 276 young girls from a government-run school in the Nigerian town of Chibok. The soldiers forced the girls to have sex with them; many were gang raped.

Women often become refugees to escape such sexual enslavement. One such refugee is Nadia Murad Basee Taha. She is Yazidi, a member of a non-Muslim Kurdish ethnic group. In 2014 when

Nadia Murad Basee Taha (far left), a survivor of sexual enslavement, talks to women in a refugee camp in Greece. In 2014 she was sold as a sex slave after ISIS militants attacked her village in Iraq and killed most of her family.

ISIS seized her village of Kocho, Iraq, it murdered six of Murad's brothers and her mother. Following this horror, Murad was sold as a sex slave to an ISIS fighter. Over the next few months, her captor and other ISIS members sexually assaulted her, sometimes several at the same time.

Murad was eventually able to escape and make her way to a refugee camp. But the horrors she endured will always haunt her. In a 2016 interview she said, "I never thought in my life, I'd be sold. It's painful to say, as a human, 'I was sold.'"[26] Murad still thinks about other women she knew who were forced to become sex slaves. Murad also thinks about two women she knew who killed themselves rather than be sold into slavery.

Being forced to marry is another reason some women become refugees. For example, in 2016 a seventeen-year-old girl named Peace fled from her village in Nigeria to avoid being forced

The Lost Boys of Sudan

James Chiengjiek was eleven when his father was killed while fighting in South Sudan's civil war. Two years later he ran away from home. Young boys like him were being kidnapped and forced to fight in the war. "Even if you are 10 years old they can recruit you to join them," says Chiengjiek. "I saw that I wasn't well enough to join the army, so I ran away." In doing so, he become one of an estimated twenty thousand young men age seven to seventeen who became separated from their families due to the war. They are known today as the Lost Boys of Sudan.

Many Lost Boys tried to travel elsewhere in Africa or even to Europe or the United States. They walked more than 1,000 miles (1,609 km) through other war zones, and it is estimated that half of them died on the journey. Those who survived spent the next several years in refugee camps.

Chiengjiek was one of these survivors. He made it to the Kakuma Refugee Camp, a Kenyan facility run by the UNHCR. Eventually, he took up running, a popular activity in Kenya. He became good at it and realized he might be able to become a professional athlete. "If God gives you a talent, you have to use it," he says. He excelled in numerous competitions and eventually joined the Refugee Olympic Team to compete in the 2016 Summer Olympics.

Patrick Marché, "Olympic Refugee Team: James Chiengjiek's Escape from the Clutches of War to Rio 2016," Rio 2016, June 9, 2016. www.rio2016.com.

to marry a forty-year-old man. "This man took me to his house and made me his house girl," she reports. "I said to my aunt, 'He's older than my dad,' but she said, 'If you don't marry this man, I will poison you.'"[27] Because even her relatives backed the marriage, Peace felt she had no choice but to leave. She made it first to an African refugee camp and then to one in Palermo, Italy. The journey that Peace and other refugees make does not end when they reach a new country, however. It is an ongoing experience, one that requires them to relearn almost everything in order to start their lives anew.

Chapter 3

The Harsh Reality of Refugee Life

Focus Questions

1. Refugees encounter many dangers on their journey. Of these, which do you think are most threatening, and why? Name at least two.
2. Many people become refugees because they fear they will be killed if they do not leave their homes. What would make you leave your home, friends, and everything you love to move somewhere else? Do you think you would have enough courage to do that? Explain your answer.
3. Would you be willing to welcome refugees who came to your country or community? Would you be willing to let them into your country but not your community? Explain your reasoning.

Most citizens live in countries where their government guarantees them basic human rights that are globally recognized. These include equality and equal treatment under the law regardless of race, religion, gender, or country of origin; freedom of speech; and freedom to travel and live where one wants. Some people become refugees precisely because their country does not guarantee them such rights. This makes them vulnerable to being victimized in a variety of ways.

Refugees suffer many types of violence and abuse. In war zones soldiers fighting on either side of a conflict may attack them if they are mistaken for the enemy. Criminals often rob, kill, and sexually assault refugees, even children. Some nations prevent refugees from crossing their borders, regardless of whether they want to settle in the nation or just travel through it. Many are forced into refugee camps against their will because the nations they have reached do not know what to do with them. Such camps often lack food, water, and housing and feature brutal or abusive treatment by those living in and in charge of the camp.

UN Special Adviser Adama Dieng says the suffering that refugees endure is similar to the atrocities that take place during war. "During their journey to Europe and other locations, many refugees have witnessed or been victims of crimes and human rights violations, including murder and enforced disappearance, slavery and extortion, sexual violence, torture and other forms of cruel, inhumane and degrading treatment,"[28] he says. Although Dieng has promised that the UN and various government agencies will try to stop such mistreatment, the reality is that millions of people face hardship and danger from the moment they leave their home.

Leaving Home

Just trying to flee war and persecution is dangerous. ISIS fighters have killed people for trying to escape from cities it controls. Azal Obaid, a government official in Iraq's Anbar Province, says that in April 2016 ISIS burned fifteen people to death for trying to leave Fallujah. In June 2016 several families had to hide in a marshy area for four days before successfully escaping from that city. During that time, thirty-two men, women, and children who feared being captured by ISIS soldiers survived on unclean marsh water and stale dates.

Many refugees lack basic necessities like food and water. They often flee their homes so quickly that they cannot take much food with them, and anything they do manage to carry gets consumed quickly. They must also leave behind most if not all of their possessions. Sometimes refugees take only what they can carry or the clothes they are wearing. Josephine Maziku escaped civil war in South Sudan in June 2016, making it to the safety of a refugee camp in Uganda. Maziku, who was pregnant, gave birth in the camp. "I wish I had managed to carry clothes," says the eighteen-year-old mother. "At least I could use those to cover my child."[29] Similarly, a woman named Fidá fled her village in Iraq with almost nothing. She is a young Christian who left because she feared

People who have fled fighting in South Sudan live in a refugee camp in Juba. Refugees endure severe hardships and harsh living conditions. They are often forced into camps that lack adequate food, water, and housing.

ISIS would kill her and her children. "We had to start our lives from zero, since we hadn't brought much money with us when we ran away from ISIS,"[30] she says.

Some people escape in cars or other vehicles. Many others walk, like Mohammad Jumma, a janitor in Damascus who fled Syria's civil war with his family. Jumma walked for weeks with his ten-year-old daughter, Farah, slung over his shoulder. Leo Dobbs, a spokesperson for the UNHCR, attests that the journey to safety is arduous for many South Sudanese fleeing their homes. "Many refugees arrive exhausted after days walking in the bush and going without food or water,"[31] says Dobbs. Many refugees must walk hundreds of miles without enough to eat or drink, which is especially difficult for those with children or older relatives.

A Dangerous Journey

The journey for some refugees is short if they can get to a refugee camp in a nearby country. However, many must travel much farther. Refugees typically cross hundreds of thousands of miles to get from Africa and the Middle East to Europe or beyond. Each segment of the trip is often filled with peril and hardship. For example, according to a 2016 report by Doctors for Human Rights, an Italian humanitarian group that helps refugees, 90 percent of one thousand African refugees interviewed said they had seen fellow travelers beaten, killed, or die from exhaustion during their perilous journeys. Says one refugee who fled over the Sahara Desert to Libya and then paid smugglers to take him across the Mediterranean Sea to Europe, "You are no longer considered a human being on this journey."[32]

While traveling, refugees constantly fear being robbed and killed. Women, and sometimes children, face sexual assault during their journey. There are many reports of women and child refugees being taken captive by criminals and forced to work as sex slaves. For example, seventy-five women who fled civil war in Syria made it to Lebanon, only to be forced to work as prostitutes. The women were kept in a two-story home in Jounieh and were beaten and tortured if they did not make enough money. They were allowed to leave the house only for medical care (which including receiving abortions if they became pregnant). When Lebanese police freed them in April 2016, police spokesperson Joseph Mousallam said, "These 75 women were saved from slavery, real slavery in this day and age with all the meaning of the word. They had lost every aspect of their freedom, over their bodies and even their thoughts."[33]

> "You are no longer considered a human being on this journey."[32]
>
> —A refugee who fled over the Sahara Desert to Libya

Some countries have tried to close their borders to refugees because they do not want the expense of caring for them or because they reject them due to their religion, race, or ethnic background. For example, due to geography, many African and Middle Eastern refugees go first to Turkey to get to Europe. After being overwhelmed by thousands of refugees in 2016, Turkey began to use violence to keep them out. News outlets reported that Turkish border guards were shooting refugees, and one story claimed that at least sixteen migrants had been killed over a four-month period. "Turkish soldiers used to help the refugees across, carry their bags for them," says one man who had previously helped people travel into Turkey. "Now they shoot at them."[34]

Smugglers and Refugees

Refugees might travel over land or water, and crossing either can be very dangerous. Part of the danger comes from relying on smugglers, who help refugees cross borders illegally. The flow of refugees to Europe exploded in 2015. The International Organization for Migration reports that more than 1 million people arrived in Europe by sea that year, while nearly thirty-five thousand came by land. Those figures, however, do not include people who arrived undetected. Smugglers play a key role in helping such refugees get to Europe.

Many refugees pay smugglers to take them over particularly dangerous stretches of land and water. Smugglers are often used to cross the Sahara, for example, which is one path to Europe from North Africa. This is a dangerous journey because of the desert's scalding temperatures and lack of water. Smugglers supposedly have supplies stashed throughout their journey or may have made arrangements with people who live along the route, allowing refugees to safely cross private or hostile territory. However, smugglers often pose a threat to the refugees in their care. Some have reportedly sold refugees into slavery; others have inadvertently caused their death. In 2015 a smuggler known as Cisse, who regularly transported refugees by truck, told British journalist Patrick Kingsley that some refugees transported by smugglers died when their vehicles broke down or ran out of gas or when drivers became lost in the desert's shifting sands.

Refugees face similar dangers trying to get to Europe by sea. Because it is illegal to enter Europe without permission, refugees pay smugglers to take them there. However, thousands of refugees have died when their smugglers' small boats and rafts sank

"It's ridiculous. Three hundred passengers is the maximum for a seventeen-meter (18.6-yard-long) boat. But people are sending out boats loaded with 350, 700, 800 [people]."[35]

—Haji, a smuggler, on boats overcrowded with refugees

or capsized. Because smugglers are paid per person they transport, they often load more people onto vessels than is safe. "It's ridiculous," admitted a smuggler called Haji. "Three hundred passengers is the maximum for a seventeen-meter (18.6-yard-long) boat. But people are sending out boats loaded with 350, 700, 800 [people]."[35]

Traveling in such crowded boats is very dangerous. On September 21, 2016, at least 162 people died when their boat sank off the coast of Egypt, a popular jumping off point to Europe. Survivors claimed overcrowding was to blame. Ahmed Darwish, a survivor, says, "My advice is that no one should undertake this risk, and especially anyone who saw these things, they will never do it again."[36] Another such incident occurred on October 3, 2013, when more than 360 people died when their boat sailing from Libya to Italy sank off the coast of Lampedusa, an Italian island. Such lives have been lost despite massive efforts by European countries to rescue refugees. In early October 2016, for example, the Italian

The Little Boy Who Shocked the World

On September 2, 2015, three-year-old Aylan Kurdi of Syria unwittingly became the face of a growing global refugee crisis. Aylan's family had fled the war in Syria, and he drowned when their inflatable boat sank before it could reach Turkey. Turkish photojournalist Nilufer Demir took a picture of Aylan lying facedown in the sand on the shore of the Mediterranean Sea near Bodrum, Turkey. He was wearing a red T-shirt, blue shorts, and cheap plastic shoes.

Over the next few days, the tragic picture appeared in numerous newspapers and magazines and went viral on Facebook and other social media. It touched the hearts of millions of people, making them aware for the first time of refugees' suffering. Demir says she took the picture to show the world the harsh reality of refugee life. "The only thing I could do was make his outcry heard," says Demir. Cheryl Newman is director of photography for the *Telegraph*, the British newspaper that published the photo. She explains why it was so powerful: "It is impossible to forget once you've looked at it. Even if you shut your eyes immediately, it's too late. The image is with you. It will remain in your memory forever."

Quoted in Robert Chalmers, "How the Aylan Kurdi Pictures Fit into the History of World-Changing Images," *Newsweek*, September 23, 2015. www.newsweek.com.

navy and coast guard rescued more than 11,000 refugees from the Mediterranean Sea in just two days. The recovery effort also found at least 50 people who had died, including 20 who had suffocated in the hold of an overcrowded boat. The International Organization for Migration reported that in 2015 more than 3,770 people died trying to cross the Mediterranean Sea, most of whom were traveling from northern Africa to Italy. More than 800 died in the Aegean Sea as they traveled from Turkey to Greece.

Smugglers also take advantage of refugees who cannot afford the cost of passage by making them work to pay off their trip. In Libya men and young boys have reportedly been forced to take backbreaking jobs in construction and agriculture for less than $5 a day. They had to work until they earned the $1,500 passage fee. Women sometimes resort to prostitution to afford their trips.

Even after a difficult and dangerous journey, many refugees wind up short of their destination because some nations force them into refugee camps. Here their lives can be as harsh and miserable as the ones they just escaped.

Refugee Camps

Many nations set up camps to house refugees until they can either return to their homeland or are granted asylum, which is permission to move permanently to another country. Many refugee camps have been in operation for decades. The Kakuma Refugee Camp in Kenya opened in 1991 to host refugees from all over Africa. The Dadaab camp in Kenya opened a year later. By 2016 it had become the world's largest camp, with a population of more than three hundred thousand. Some refugee camps were set up with the intention to house people for years. Many others, particularly those in Europe, were designed very quickly to cope with the massive numbers of people suddenly arriving.

Many camps—especially ones built very quickly—have routinely been condemned for failing to provide decent living conditions. These include little or no opportunities for education; lack of access to sanitation facilities; inadequate shelter, food, and

Many refugee camps have been condemned for failing to provide decent living conditions, particularly lacking proper sanitation, food and water supplies, and medical care. This severely malnourished seven-month-old boy receives treatment in a field hospital in Dadaab, Kenya.

medical care; and the risk of experiencing violence and sexual abuse. In some camps, refugees live in tents or out in the open. In others, they are housed in vacant warehouses, factories, or other large buildings that are not suitable for habitation.

Some of the worst conditions have been reported at a camp in Nauru, a small island nation near Australia that cooperates with Australia to house refugees from Iraq, Afghanistan, Bangladesh, Pakistan, and Burma. In August 2016 the *Guardian* newspaper published an article on the camp's abuse of young people it had compiled from more than two thousand incident reports. These included guards threatening to kill children and sexually assaulting them. There were also reports of children harming themselves to cope with the trauma, such as one girl who sewed her own lips together. "The Nauru files set out as never before the assaults, sexual abuse, self-harm attempts, child abuse and living conditions endured by asylum seekers held by the Australian government, painting a picture of routine dysfunction and cruelty,"[37] the newspaper reported.

Passing Time in a Refugee Camp

Habib is a refugee who fled Afghanistan to escape that country's ongoing violence. In 2016 he was living in a refugee camp in Greece. His new home was a baseball stadium that housed thousands of refugees. Habib describes how boring and meaningless life was in the camp:

> You wake up in the morning. We look at each other. There's nothing. Then we go and have breakfast. Then we come back and sit and look at each other. There's nothing else. We used to have some playing cards, and then somebody stole it. So we try to listen to music on the cell phones. And then we look at each other again. And then it's afternoon. Then we go and have some lunch. And then we come back and sit here and then look at each other again. And then we just fall asleep. We take a long nap until 6:00 PM. And then at 6:00 PM, we go and play some soccer. And then we come back here, have dinner. And then we look at each other again, and then we fall asleep. . . . On normal days, regular days, one hour to us passes like one whole year of boredom.

Quoted in Uri Friedman, "The UN's Urgent Plan to Help Refugees—Two Years from Now," *Atlantic*, September 20, 2016. www.theatlantic.com.

In addition to these hardships, in many camps there is nothing to do. Boredom can be difficult to deal with, says Sanna, a seventeen-year-old who fled the African nation of Gambia. "This place is very difficult," he says of conditions in his refugee camp in Pozzallo, Italy. "We are not at school—if we were, we could say we have a normal life. But we are here, and all we do is eat and sit. They had a football [soccer ball] before, but the ball is flat now."[38] In other camps, however, it is possible for refugees to have positive experiences. Esther Nyakong arrived in Kakuma in 2009 after she, her mother, and her two sisters fled civil war in South Sudan. In 2015, after living at Kakuma for six years, seventeen-year-old Esther excelled at school. She loved science and math, and her goal was to become South Sudan's first female neurosurgeon.

> "In Lesbos, we understood that we were stuck in a place that we could not leave, [we were] in a trap, a prison."[40]
>
> —Hasan, a Syrian, on living in a refugee camp in Greece

Esther says she began to study hard because "my mother had given up and I was afraid that she did not have any hope left in life."[39] Seeing Esther get an education made her mother happy, and that made Esther happy.

Getting Out

Most camp experiences are negative, and refugees seek to leave camps as soon as possible. However, gaining permission to move to another country is a difficult process, one that can drag on for months or years. Refugees who want to establish themselves elsewhere often become depressed during this time. Hasan is an engineer from Damascus, Syria, who made it to a camp in Lesbos, Greece, with his wife, Nour, and their two-year-old son. "In Lesbos, we understood that we were stuck in a place that we could not leave, [we were] in a trap, a prison."[40] After nearly a year of traveling and several months spent in a refugee camp, in April 2016 Hasan and his family finally got lucky. After visiting the camp, Pope Francis granted asylum in Italy to three refugee families, Hasan's among them. Hasan called the pope a savior for giving them a chance at a new life. If Francis had not helped them, their wait would have been much longer.

Even when individuals manage to leave a camp, they often cannot enjoy their freedom. Along the way, they have lost the people most important to them. Indeed, throughout the refugee journey, family members often get separated from each other, including children from their parents. Once separated it is hard to reunite with loved ones, because there is no coordinated system by which to make such searches. When family members are reunited, it is cause for much celebration. For example, in 2016 two brothers from Afghanistan were reunited in a refugee camp in Calais, France. Noor, twenty-two, and Alam, sixteen, had fled Afghanistan after their father was killed in fighting several years earlier. They became separated after leaving their homeland; Noor made it to the United Kingdom, and Alam wound up in Calais. They eventually found each other with the help of a British radio station, and when they finally met again, they could not stop hugging each other. "I'm so happy," says Noor. "Now I know I'll enjoy my life. I found my family."[41]

Chapter 4

Beginning Anew

Focus Questions

1. Imagine you were starting life anew in a different country. What would you feel compelled to do first? Explain your answer.

2. Refugees are often rejected or treated with hostility by people in countries where they seek asylum. Why do you think some people reject refugees? Do you think it is fair or warranted to do so? Why or why not?

3. Do you think the arrival of refugees in your country would help or hurt its development or economic growth? Explain your reasoning.

From 2015 through 2016 the United States admitted ten thousand refugees from the ongoing civil war in Syria. Among these were Mahmoud Kabati; his wife, Nareesa; and their two children; who began new lives in Michigan. The Kabatis fled Syria in 2011, and their long journey to the United States included three and a half years in a refugee camp in Jordan. When the family arrived in Dearborn, Michigan, in June 2016, Nareesa was grateful for the chance to stop moving. "We've been homeless for five years," she said. "It's time to finally settle down."[42] Among the family members' goals was to learn to speak English so they could communicate with Americans and integrate into US culture.

The language barrier is but one of many obstacles refugees face when they settle in a new place. To have a chance at a new life, refugees must first overcome one of the greatest challenges facing them—being accepted into another country.

Refugee Status and Asylum

Refugees are people who have left their home nations and cannot return because of war or persecution. When they finally get to a new country, they become known as asylum seekers. Asylum seekers are refugees who have applied for refugee status from a particular nation so they can live there. Rules on asylum vary from nation to nation. In the United States people who are granted asylum are allowed to work and can apply for a green card so they can live there permanently.

> "Refugees should receive at least the same rights and basic help as any other foreigner who is a legal resident, including freedom of thought, of movement, and freedom from torture and degrading treatment."[43]
>
> —A 2002 UN document on refugee rights

The definition of refugee and asylum status, and the rights and privileges refugees should be given by a nation, are spelled out in a 1951 UN agreement that has been accepted by more than 140 countries. In 2002 the UN reaffirmed the right refugees have to safe asylum in other countries. It noted that refugees are entitled to physical security from harm and laid out the basic human rights that nations are expected to give people who live in their country. The UNHCR states: "Refugees should receive at least the same rights and basic help as any other foreigner who is a legal resident, including freedom of thought, of movement, and freedom from torture and degrading treatment. Economic and social rights are equally applicable. Refugees should have access to medical care, schooling and the right to work."[43]

However, it can take months or even years to gain asylum, especially when there are huge numbers of refugees seeking it at one time. Before being accepted into a country, refugees must undergo lengthy and detailed interviews, background checks to confirm their identity, and assessments on whether they will be safe in their new homeland. The process is long, invasive, and emotionally draining. Refugees struggle through time-consuming interviews in which they are grilled about their past, their beliefs, and what they hope to do in the future. Those who are rejected can appeal the decision, but that takes even longer. The amount of time that a man named Amir and his wife, Walaa—teachers who fled the civil war in Syria—spent waiting for asylum was torturous. They waited six months on the Greek island of Chios for their request for asylum to be approved. Amir said that every day that they were denied acceptance was like dying because it killed their hopes and dreams for a better future. "I know in Syria we have war and bombs every day, every Syrian dies once," he said. "Here we die every day. Every day is bad."[44]

One reason it takes so long to be approved is that so many refugees come from nations like Syria, Iraq, and Afghanistan that have also produced terrorists. European nations and the United States are worried that they will be unable to tell the asylum seekers from would-be terrorists. For example, in 2016 terrorist attacks

A family from Syria adjusts to their new life in Dearborn, Michigan. Between 2015 and 2016 the United States admitted ten thousand refugees from Syria.

were committed in France, Belgium, and the United States by followers of ISIS. One of the most prominent US terrorist attacks in recent years came December 2, 2015, when Syed Rizwan Farook and Tashfeen Malik, a married couple of Pakistani descent, killed fourteen people and injured twenty-two others by shooting them in San Bernardino, California. They were killed themselves in a shootout with police. These violent episodes cause many people to view refugees from such countries with suspicion. It also slows down the process of vetting peaceful asylum seekers and separating them from those who might have bad intentions and suspicious connections.

Education Is Scarce

When a refugee finally gets permission to move to a new country, he or she faces many other problems. One of the biggest is a lack of opportunity for education, at all levels. Refugees need a wide variety of educational opportunities when they arrive in a new nation. Their first task is to learn the local language so they can look for work and function in society. This was the challenge facing Sanas Somijara, a teenager from Afghanistan who was accepted into Germany in 2016. "I didn't know a word of German when I got to Berlin,"[45] says the fifteen-year-old. But Somijara spoke English, which helped her learn to read and write German because she was familiar with the Roman alphabet that both languages use. She says learning is much harder for Middle Eastern refugees who know only Arabic script.

In addition to learning the language, refugees must also go to school. However, host nations have limited funds to help refugees with their schooling. "When donations fall short and the money is tight, education is the first item on the list of refugees' needs that gets crossed off,"[46] says Melissa Fleming, head of communications and public information for the UNHCR. The result is that in 2016 only half of all refugees worldwide attended primary school. Just one in four attended secondary school (high school), and only one in one hundred went to college.

In 2016 Germany led European nations in accepting refugees; it admitted about 890,000 men, women, and children, and has a system set up to educate refugees within its borders. School-age refugees first attend introductory classes in German primary

From Afghanistan to Great Britain

Gulwali Passarlay was twelve in 2006 when his mother paid smugglers $8,000 to take him from Afghanistan to Europe so the Taliban could not force him to become a suicide bomber. In his 2016 book, *The Lightless Sky: A Twelve-Year-Old Refugee's Harrowing Escape from Afghanistan and His Extraordinary Journey Across Half the World*, Passarlay recounted his yearlong trip to Great Britain. His journey included being arrested by police, jumping from a speeding train, and almost drowning off the coast of Greece. The final ordeal was when British officials questioned him when he sought asylum. For nearly a year they refused to believe he was from Afghanistan and only thirteen (they insisted he was older). They refused to let him stay in Great Britain. Passarlay says of that experience:

> I went through hell. My age was disputed. My nationality was disputed, which was the biggest insult. There's nothing worse than not being believed by the authorities and social services. I came to the conclusion that life was not worth living [and] I wanted to commit suicide. I was like, "What is the point of life if no one believes you? I crossed half the world for what? Am I not a human being?"

Passarlay eventually won asylum and, with the help of government programs and a foster family, was able to make a new life for himself.

Quoted in Michael Petro, "The Interview: Gulwali Passarlay on His Escape from Afghanistan," *Maclean's*, January 7, 2016. www.macleans.ca.

and secondary schools to prepare them for regular school. Germany has set aside $2.55 billion for courses for about 350,000 school-age refugees who entered the country in 2015. School is challenging for these students, because in addition to contending with a language barrier, many of them may not have attended school for a long time. Years may have passed since they fled their home and school. "I have some pupils who have been out of school for three or four years while they were fleeing their home country," says Guido Siegel, who teaches refugee students in Berlin. "They have problems and learn very slowly."[47]

Educational opportunities are much more limited or even nonexistent in refugee camps and in other countries that accept refugees. By October 2016 Mohammed Zaitoon, a Syrian refugee in Greece, had not been to school for more than a year. "I'm sad because I don't have school now," he said. "And I want to go to school."[48] Zaitoon was one of an estimated twenty thousand school-age children in Greek refugee camps. Greece tried to persuade school districts near the camps to accept refugees, but many refused, citing religious and cultural differences as well as the fear that refugees might be carrying diseases that could infect Greek children (though this was never proven).

Finding Work

Another immediate challenge facing a refugee is to find work. Many refugees have trouble getting hired because they lack education or do not have the skills employers need. Refugees from very poor countries are also disadvantaged in finding work because they are not familiar with modern technology such as computers, the Internet, or smartphones. However, even refugees who are educated and have professional training have trouble

A refugee from Afghanistan apprentices at a car manufacturer in Germany. Germany has led European nations in accepting refugees.

finding jobs in their field because they have no way to prove their education, skills, and work history.

One such refugee is Abdelbary Alsado, who was a pathologist in Raqqa, Syria, and owned his own medical laboratory. After ISIS occupied Raqqa in 2013, Alsado fled with his family to Turkey, then Greece, and eventually Canada. Without paperwork to prove he had once been a doctor, Alsado worked first for a Pizza Hut and then as a lab assistant in a hospital. Despite being overqualified for such low-level positions, the former doctor says, "I think I was lucky [to have a job]"[49] because so many refugees cannot find work at all.

Many refugees must learn new skills, and some governments and business organizations are finding ways to help them do so. One example comes from Finland, where the software development company Integrify teaches refugees computer coding even though many of them have never used computers before. Schools in other European countries are helping make refugees more employable. In February 2016 Facebook cofounder Mark Zuckerberg visited a coding school in Berlin, Germany. After the experience, he posted, "Dealing with the refugee crisis is a huge challenge, and it is inspiring to see people creating opportunities through technology."[50]

Despite such training programs, many refugees struggle to find work, for several reasons. In Germany, for example, refugees are restricted from working immediately after entering the country and are allowed only to accept jobs that German citizens have turned down. Job conditions vary from nation to nation, but historically it has been easier for refugees to work in the United States, where they are allowed to apply for jobs immediately after they begin living there. David Bier, an immigration policy analyst for the Cato Institute, says, "By comparison [with Germany], the United States rapidly incorporates refugees into the labor market."[51] Groups like the International Rescue Committee (IRC) help with this task. The IRC helps refugees find housing, learn English, and develop job skills. The group also partners with local organizations and businesses to hire refugees. "Our program really focuses on self-sufficiency," says Nicky Walker, an IRC official in Phoenix, Arizona. "We want to make sure that people know and understand how to get a job."[52]

Fear and Rejection

Another significant challenge facing refugees involves the way the citizens of their new country will receive them. People often fear what is different—and many refugees are quite different from the people of their host country. For example, Asmaa al-Bukaie fled from Syria to Egypt in 2013 and wound up living in Boise, Idaho. Her traditional religious clothing, a shawl-like head covering, easily identified her as Muslim. At first al-Bukaie enjoyed living in Boise because it was a place of freedom and safety. But after a while she noticed people were staring at her in a hostile way. "I feel like probably I am in danger because I start to see people acting differently [toward] . . . Muslim women or Muslim with a scarf,"[53] she says. When one of her sons was punched in the face for admitting he was Muslim, she began to worry Boise was no longer a safe place to live.

That some in her community were suspicious of al-Bukaie because of the way she looks is something refugees in other nations also deal with. On July 5, 2016, Emmanuel Chidi Namdi, a Nigerian asylum seeker, was beaten to death in Fermo, Italy, after he reacted angrily to a man who called his wife a monkey. The couple was Christian and had fled Nigeria after the terrorist group Boko Haram attacked their church and killed their friends and relatives. Although Italian prime minister Matteo Renzi condemned the murder and any other hatred, racism, or violence toward refugees, violence continues to be directed toward refugees in Italy and elsewhere. For example, Austria reported twenty-five attacks on refugee centers in the first half of 2016, one more than occurred in all of 2015. In November 2016 dozens of people were driven out of the Souda refugee camp on the Greek island of Chios after two nights of violent attacks. Attackers hurled Molotov cocktails and boulders from elevated areas surrounding the camp. Three tents were burned and several people injured, including a Nigerian boy who was hit by a rock. "We do not have any kind of protection," said Syrian refugee Mostafa al-Khatib. "No one cares about us."[54]

> "I feel like probably I am in danger because I start to see people acting differently [toward] . . .
> Muslim women or Muslim with a scarf."[53]
>
> —Asmaa Al-Bukaie, who now lives in Boise, Idaho, is worried about fear of Muslim refugees being terrorists

Syrian children attend class in a public school in El Cajon, California. Although many refugees face rejection and even attacks from those who think they are a threat to their way of life, the majority of Americans believe that greater diversity in a nation makes it a better place to live.

Attacks like these are driven by the fear people often have of refugees. For example, a 2016 Pew Research Center survey of people in ten European nations found that 59 percent believed the arrival of so many refugees increased their nation's risk of terrorist attack. The survey showed terrorism fears were driven by negative views people had of Muslim refugees. In addition, the majority of respondents thought the diversity that refugees offered their nation would hurt daily life. In the United States, however, 58 percent of people polled felt the greater diversity refugees brought to the nation would make it a better place to live.

John Birky is a doctor who is helping create a medical clinic for refugees. While some people fear refugees because they worry they will commit terrorist attacks, Birky thinks the truth is that refugees often flee their homeland to get *away* from extremists and terrorists. Birky urges Americans to understand that refugees are "trying to make a better life for their families here. They want to pursue the American dream."[55]

Always a Refugee?

For these reasons, some refugees believe they will never be totally accepted in their new homelands. One such person is Ali, who at age seventeen made it to the island of Lesbos, Greece, with his younger brother, Ahmed, after a sea journey in an overcrowded raft. Their parents had sent them away from their home in Lebanon to protect them from rising danger there. In September 2016 Ali, who now lives in Germany, said life was better for him in many ways. But Ali worries he might always bear the stigma of being a refugee. "As a refugee, there is always a sense of feeling inferior to others,"[56] he said.

A Plot to Kill Somali Refugees in Kansas

On October 15, 2016, three men in Garden City, Kansas, were arrested for planning to bomb an apartment building where Somali refugees lived. The men were members of a militia group called the Crusaders that opposes the resettlement of Muslims and other refugees in their community. Their arrest capped an eight-month FBI investigation into the group.

During the investigation, a confidential FBI source attended the group's meetings in southwestern Kansas and learned of the violent plan. The men were charged with conspiring to use a weapon of mass destruction; if convicted they could be sentenced to life in federal prison without parole.

The plot to kill Somalis was just one of a series of hate crimes across the United States fueled by fear of Muslim refugees. Among those shocked and dismayed by news of the plot was Nihad Awad, who heads the Council on American-Islamic Relations. "We ask our nation's political leaders, and particularly political candidates, to reject the growing Islamophobia in our nation," Awad says.

Quoted in CBS News, "Militia Members Arrested in Alleged Plot Targeting Muslims," October 15, 2016. www.cbs news.com.

However, Syrian refugees Motab Al-Ali, his wife, and their five children regard their new home in the United States as what they have long hoped for. They escaped the war-torn city of Aleppo and since December 2015 have lived in Pittsburgh. Motab works sorting packages for FedEx. His children attend school and are very happy with their new life. "I'm looking at myself as an American now,"[57] says Motab. His wife, Sabha, reports she is just as happy. "I'm alive," she says. "My babies are alive."[58] Iman, their youngest child, was born in Pittsburgh in February 2016 as a US citizen. The entire family hopes to join him as US citizens in the future.

> "I'm looking at myself as an American now."[57]
>
> —Motab Al-Ali, a Syrian refugee who now lives in Pittsburgh

Chapter 5

Dealing Humanely with Refugees

Focus Questions
1. Upon moving to a new country, what kind of help do you think refugees most need? Why?
2. To what extent do you think your nation should help refugees who move to your country? What kind of help do you think is most appropriate to extend? Include specific examples in your answer.
3. Has your nation or state taken in refugees in recent years? If so, do you think they have been treated fairly or unfairly? Explain your answer.

There has been mixed global response to the plight of the 21 million refugees who have fled their homelands because of persecution and war. Some countries have generously helped and accepted refugees. Others have been criticized for weakly responding to their needs. Still others have refused to help them entirely. Given this mixed response, in 2016 world leaders held two summits to discuss how to better address the largest refugee crisis since World War II. President Barack Obama declared that the world's nations, including his own, needed to do more to meet the humanitarian needs of millions of men, women, and children. "It's a test of our international system where all nations ought to share in our collective responsibilities," he said. "We cannot avert our eyes or turn our backs. To slam the door in the face of these families would betray our deepest values."[59]

The meetings brought new commitments from participating nations to resettle or admit 360,000 refugees over the next year, twice as many as they had the previous year. From October 1, 2015, until September 30, 2016 the United States admitted 85,000 refugees, including a record number of Muslims: 38,901. Obama pledged that in the next fiscal year beginning October 1, 2016, his nation would accept 110,000 more refugees from around the world. However when Donald Trump was elected president in 2016, he vowed to reduce immigration. More than fifty nations and charitable and humanitarian organizations also promised to increase funding for refugees by $4.5 billion in the coming year.

But Kenneth Roth, executive director of Human Rights Watch, says there was something even more powerful that countries could do to help refugees: guarantee that they are protected by the human rights that are mandated by international standards. Rights refugees are often denied include being prevented from traveling where they want, being safe from physical harm, and having adequate housing, medical care, and educational opportunities. In Roth's opinion, countries could help refugees by making sure they are granted the rights afforded them by international agreements like the Universal Declaration of Human Rights. "Millions of lives hang in the balance," says Roth. "This is not just about more money or greater resettlement numbers, but also about shoring up the legal principles for protecting refugees, which are under threat as never before."[60]

> "We cannot avert our eyes or turn our backs. To slam the door in the face of these families would betray our deepest values."[59]
>
> —Barack Obama, forty-fourth US president

The Global Response

Amnesty International reports that as of October 2016 more than half the world's refugees were being cared for in only 10 of the world's 193 nations. Turkey has the most refugees, with 2.5 million. Pakistan hosts 1.6 million, and Lebanon hosts 1.1 million. Other countries that have willingly housed large numbers of refugees include Iran, Jordan, Ethiopia, Kenya, Uganda, and the Democratic Republic of the Congo. Several of those host countries are also among the poorest in the world, making it difficult

This Congolese couple and their children were resettled in Montana. In 2016 the US government admitted 85,000 refugees and pledged to increase that figure to 110,000 in the next fiscal year, ending September 30, 2017.

for them to care for refugees. Many wealthy nations, including the United States and most European countries, have contributed large sums of money toward the refugee problem but have taken in far fewer numbers of people. This is why people like Salil Shetty, secretary general of Amnesty International, have criticized richer nations for not doing more to help refugees. "Wealthy countries have shown a complete absence of leadership and responsibility [in the refugee crisis],"[61] he says.

In part, certain nations have hosted more refugees because of their proximity to crisis areas. Jordan has a lot of Syrian refugees because Syria is right next door. For the same reason, Pakistan hosts a lot of refugees from Afghanistan, and Kenya hosts a lot of refugees from the Sudanese civil war. However, the global refugee situation expanded in 2015, when an estimated 1.3 million people made the dangerous journey to Europe in the hopes that wealthy countries on the Continent would have more resources to help them.

Germany has accepted the most refugees of all the European nations—890,000 were resettled in Germany in 2015. Sigmar Gabriel, Germany's economy minister, says it is hoped that refugees will strengthen the German economy. Germany's working-age population is expected to decline by 6 million people by 2030, and refugees could mitigate the anticipated shortage of workers. "If we manage to quickly train those that come to us and to get them into work, then we will solve one of our biggest problems for the economic future of our country: the skills shortage,"[62] says Gabriel. Other European nations that have accepted large numbers of refugees include Hungary, which has taken in 170,000, and Sweden, which has taken in 163,000 (a greater percentage of its population than any other European nation). However, most European nations have accepted far fewer—Greece has only let in about 50,000, and Great Britain about 20,000—and others even fewer.

> "Wealthy countries have shown a complete absence of leadership and responsibility [in the refugee crisis]."[61]
>
> —Salil Shetty, secretary general of Amnesty International

There are several reasons why some nations do not want to accept or help refugees. For one, it is terrifically expensive to house, feed, and otherwise care for and absorb influxes of people. Some fear that terrorists might be hiding among the refugees who are let in or that refugees would otherwise compromise national security. Still others worry that refugees could compete with nationals for already scarce jobs, drastically change their culture, or otherwise threaten the majority population.

Refugee Backlash

Many European countries were more willing to accept refugees when they first began coming. But in 2015, when their numbers swelled to more than 1 million (compared to 280,000 in 2014), the tidal wave of newcomers frightened and angered some Europeans. Spyros Economides is a professor of international relations and European politics at the London School of Economics. He says Greeks initially helped refugees because they understood the refugees had fled their homes "out of a survival instinct [but] once these flows of people got larger [they] were seen as being a more problematic and divisive presence."[63]

As the refugees continued to flood in, some countries, such as Hungary and Bulgaria, used armed guards and physical barriers to keep them out. Not knowing how to handle so many people, other countries, such as Greece and France, herded them into camps while taking months to determine whether to allow the refugees to resettle within their borders. One camp in Calais, France, became known as the Jungle for its terrible conditions. People lived crowded on top of one another in tiny tents surrounded by barbed wire. One resident, Hassan Jibril of Sudan, said, "It is a very bad situation here." Pointing to a puddle of water filled with trash, Jibril said, "You see that? If you stay here, you can die [from disease brought on by filthy conditions]."[64] France finally closed the camp in October 2016 and sent the ten thousand people who had lived there to temporary shelters in other parts of the country.

> "It is a very bad situation here."[64]
>
> —Hassan Jibril, about a refugee camp known as the Jungle

In other countries, nationals have staged huge protests and have even physically attacked refugees. Interestingly, this has been the case in some of the nations that have taken in the most refugees, indicating that tensions are riding high between those who claim that accepting refugees is the right thing to do—and even economically beneficial—and those who claim that newcomers will hijack their culture, compromise their security, or compete for work. This

Citizens in the United Kingdom protest to highlight the refugee crisis and urge the government to accept more refugees into the country.

A Little Boy Offers Omran a Home

Omran Daqneesh is a five-year-old Syrian boy whose picture went viral in August 2016. Newspapers and magazines around the world published the image of the little boy sitting in the back of an ambulance in Aleppo, Syria. His body was covered with dirt and blood, and he appeared dazed, even frozen. Omran was injured when Aleppo was bombed in Syria's civil war.

Around the world in New York, a six-year-old boy named Alex saw the picture and wanted to help. Alex wrote President Barack Obama a letter saying Omran could live with his family and become his brother:

> Remember the boy who was picked up by the ambulance in Syria? Can you please go get him and bring him to [my home]? Park in the driveway or on the street and we will be waiting for you guys with flags, flowers, and balloons. We will give him a family and he will be our brother. Catherine, my little sister, will be collecting butterflies and fireflies for him. [Please] tell him that his brother will be Alex who is a very kind boy, just like him. Since he won't bring toys and doesn't have toys Catherine will share her big blue stripy white bunny. And I will share my bike and I will teach him how to ride it.

Quoted in Bill Chappell, "'He Will Be Our Brother': Boy, 6, Asks Obama to Bring Syrian Boy to Live with Him," National Public Radio, September 22, 2016. www.npr.org.

was the scene in 2016 in Germany, when citizens staged a series of antirefugee protests that featured racial and ethnic slurs about refugees and sometimes resulted in violence. Markus Ulbig, a German political leader, criticized one such protest in Saxony, saying, "I find it deeply shameful to see how people are being treated here."[65]

Such demonstrations have also taken place in Sweden, where citizens became hostile toward refugees after some of them committed crimes. For example, in Germany refugees were accused of committing 142,500 crimes in the first six months of 2016. These ranged from theft to rape. Some Swedes also feared refugees would weaken or change their country in negative ways. Antirefugee sentiments also played a role in the United Kingdom's 2016 vote to leave the European Union, the political and economic organization of twenty-eight European nations. The vote to leave, also known as Brexit, was in part motivated by the idea that if Britain was no longer in the European Union, it could not be forced to accept more refugees.

Resentment and fear toward refugees is not isolated to Europe. In the United States, too, the issue of whether to accept refugees played a role in the election of Donald Trump as president in 2016. Trump ran on a campaign that proposed the United States should bar Muslim refugees from entering the country—he warned that some could be terrorists. In fact, Republican governors of more than two dozen states had used the same argument in 2015 to avoid accepting Syrian refugees. However, refugees from Muslim countries, most of them women and children, have themselves fled terrorism. According to William Lacy Swing, director general of the International Organization for Migration, "It is the cruel irony that people fleeing terror are then accused of being terrorists themselves."[66]

> "I find it deeply shameful to see how people are being treated here."[65]
>
> —Markus Ulbig, a German political leader

Groups Help Refugees

While refugees have many opponents, they also have many entities that fight for their care and well-being. For example, Pope Francis has been a strong advocate for refugees, claiming that helping them is the right thing to do. In November 2016 at a mass in Malmö, Sweden, Francis said, "Blessed are those who look into the eyes of the abandoned and marginalized and show them their closeness. Blessed are those who renounce their own comfort in order to help others."[67] The same sentiment drives the work of many religious, charitable, and humanitarian groups that have taken up the cause of refugees. Foremost among these is the UNHCR, which is also known as the UN Refugee Agency.

The UNHCR helps refugees in every part of the world. In addition to providing temporary shelter, food, and medical care for people forced to leave their homes, the UNHCR helps them establish new lives in other countries. One person who has directly benefited from the agency's work is Kwizera Gasigwa, who was a police officer and farmer in the Democratic Republic of the Congo before war forced his family to flee to neighboring Uganda. A program run by the UNHCR and the Japan International Cooperation Agency helped him start farming again in Uganda. Kwizera and his wife, Nyiranzabi, were also able to start several small businesses to further support themselves. "Growing rice has enabled my family to purchase a motorcycle that I use to carry passengers," says Kwizera. "My wife has opened a grocery shop and things are looking good for my family."[68]

A number of other organizations, including the Roman Catholic group Jesuit Refugee Service, are also helping refugees. One person who has benefited from the group's work is Prabhat Adhikari, who was born in Bhutan, a southern Asian country located in the eastern Himalayas. His family and tens of thousands of others were forced to leave Bhutan in the 1990s because of their ethnicity. They were part of a group of people from Nepal who had settled in Bhutan centuries earlier. Adhikari grew up in a refugee camp in Nepal, his home a primitive hut made of bamboo and mud with no electricity or running water. He came to the United States in 2014 with his parents and younger sister. Thanks to the Jesuit Refugee Service, by 2016 the nineteen-year-old was living in Pittsburgh and attending community college. Adhikari is grateful for his new life. "A lot of things that people take for granted are

A Syrian Family Adjusts to Life in America

In 2012 restaurant owner Fouad Haj Ali was incarcerated in a Syrian prison for serving food to fighters who opposed President Bashar al-Assad. When Fouad was released after nine months, he and his wife, Rabia, and their five children fled Syria with only the clothes they were wearing. After spending years as refugees, in 2016 the family found a new home in the Chicago suburb of Aurora, Illinois.

Before the Haj Alis were allowed to move to the United States, officials thoroughly investigated their background. Family members were also interviewed repeatedly to determine whether they qualified for asylum and to make sure they were not terrorists. Fouad says that during the lengthy vetting process, officials appeared to be afraid of his family. "It was like they were scared of us. It was funny, really, because that whole time we were scared of them, too."

The family's five children are learning English so they can attend school. Rabia says that adjusting to a new language and culture is hard for her children, but she is grateful for their opportunity to get an education. "None of them find this easy, but we know this is the best place for our children. These schools will give them a chance we could never give them once the war started. That is worth everything."

Quoted in Louisa Loveluck, "In a Chicago Suburb, a Syrian Family Adjusts to Its New American Life," *Washington Post,* September 20, 2016. www.washingtonpost.com.

things that we have to fight really hard for," he says. "And obviously I'm thankful to all the organizations (that helped us) and for Americans for accepting us."[69]

Individuals Help Refugees

Whether as volunteers in large organizations or working on their own, many individuals are welcoming refugees into their homelands. Some are even welcoming refugees into their own homes. Gulwali Passarlay was twelve in 2006 when his mother paid smugglers to take him and his brother from Afghanistan to Europe so he would not have to join the Taliban, the Islamic fundamentalist political group that has ruled parts of Afghanistan on and off for decades. Over the next year he was separated from his brother, jailed several times, and went through many hardships before finally reaching Great Britain. Luckily for Passarlay, a family accepted him as a foster child, which changed his entire life. "My foster [family] gave me a home with love and warmth but also a cultural fast track which allowed me to better navigate my school life," he says. "Eventually I won a place at Manchester University."[70]

A similar story comes from Kaysville, Utah, when Kasey and Katie Pearce agreed to foster a teenage girl from the Democratic Republic of the Congo. When the girl arrived in December 2015, the Pearces found out she was pregnant. She gave birth to a daughter, Kisha, on July 14, 2016. The Pearces, who already had four young children, gladly accepted them both. Says Katie, "We couldn't be happier [with] how it all turned out."[71]

When Christopher Lwenzya and his family moved into a new home in Appleton, Wisconsin, on October 30, 2016, he owed a debt of gratitude to area high school students who helped build it. About 250 students from nearby high schools participated in the city's School Youth Build Partnership, which for a decade has built homes for people who need housing. Lwenzya originally fled fighting in the Democratic Republic of the Congo. "For years, I didn't have a place to call home," he says. "I just lived as if I was in transit, waiting for a place to call home. Now I feel at home."[72]

What Does the Future Hold for Refugees?

The flow of refugees began to slow toward the end of 2016, dropping from more than 1 million in all of 2015 to just 368,928 for 2016 (through November). However, ongoing problems in the Middle East, Africa, South America, and other parts of the world will continue to force people from homes for years to come.

Filippo Grandi is the United Nations High Commissioner for Refugees. He hopes that in the future, nations will treat refugees more fairly because of an agreement reached in 2016 at the UN summit on refugees. The agreement offers more financial aid for refugees and reaffirms their human rights. However, Grandi and many others hope the agreement is just the beginning. "The world—shocked by images of people fleeing in huge numbers and dying at sea—does not want our intentions to remain on paper," he says. "It demands practical action and results."[73] Only time will tell if the agreement improves the plight of refugees.

Source Notes

Introduction: Seeking New Lives

1. Quoted in Gabe Joselow, "Team Refugees: 5 Remarkable Journeys to Rio 2016 Olympic Games," NBC News, August 3, 2016. www.nbcnews.com.
2. Quoted in Patrick Kingsley, "'Prisoners of Europe': The Everyday Humiliation of Refugees Stuck in Greece," *Guardian* (Manchester), September 6, 2016. www.theguardian.com.
3. Quoted in Office of the United Nations High Commissioner for Human Rights, "Fact Sheet No. 20, Human Rights and Refugees," July 1993. www.ohchr.org.

Chapter 1: A Global Problem

4. Quoted in Patrice Taddonio, "How Four Child Refugees Said Goodbye to Syria," *Frontline*, PBS, April 19, 2016. www.pbs.org.
5. Quoted in Patrick Kingsley et al., "'I Didn't Think I Might Never See My Parents Again'—Refugee Children Share Their Stories," *Guardian* (Manchester), January 26, 2016. www.theguardian.com.
6. Quoted in Office of the United Nations High Commissioner for Human Rights, "Fact Sheet No. 20, Human Rights and Refugees."
7. Quoted in Susmita Baral, "Refugee Crisis 2016 in Europe: Death Toll and Migrant Arrival Increases, Statistics Show," *International Business Times*, August 10, 2016. www.ibtimes.com.
8. Quoted in Scott Anderson, "Fractured Lands," *New York Times Magazine*, August 11, 2016. www.nytimes.com.
9. David Francis, "How Saddam Hussein Made the Middle East Stable," *Fiscal Times*, August 26, 2013. www.thefiscaltimes.com.

10. Quoted in BBC, "Syria Conflict: The Suffering Civilians of West Aleppo," June 16, 2014. www.bbc.com.

11. Quoted in Bill Donahue, "Refugee Yiech Pur Biel Has Run His Entire Life, but Now He's a Runner," ESPN, August 9, 2016. www.espn.com.

12. Quoted in *U.S. News & World Report*, "Transcript: President Obama at the Leaders Summit on Refugees," September 20, 2016. www.usnews.com.

13. Quoted in Maya Rhodan, "President Obama: U.S. Will Accept 110,000 Refugees from Around the World," *Time*, September 20, 2016. http://time.com.

14. Quoted in Nick Bryant, "UN Focuses on Refugees—Will It Be Enough?," BBC, September 19, 2016. www.bbc.com.

Chapter 2: Why People Become Refugees

15. Quoted in Jesuit Refugee Service, "World Refugee Day: 'No Situation Is Permanent,'" June 20, 2016. http://jrsusa.org.

16. Quoted in Salam Rizk, "Living Under ISIS Rule—and Then Escaping It," PRI, February 24, 2016. www.pri.org.

17. Quoted in Jesuit Refugee Service, "Eritrean Refugee Faces Challenges with Grace," June 27, 2016. http://jrsusa.org.

18. Quoted in Nicholas Johansen, "Gay Refugee Sponsored," Castanet, September 19, 2016. www.castanet.net.

19. Quoted in Carolyn Thompson, "'I Keep Hoping to See Them': Tamma Joyce, 19, Separated from Family Fleeing South Sudan Bloodshed," CBC News, September 25, 2016. www.cbc.ca.

20. Daniel Byman, "After the Hope of the Arab Spring, the Chill of an Arab Winter," *Washington Post*, December 1, 2011. www.washingtonpost.com.

21. Quoted in Patrick Kingsley, *The New Odyssey: The Story of Europe's Refugee Crisis*. London: Guardian Faber, 2016, p. 22.

22. Quoted in Philip Issa and Edith M. Lederer, "At Least 26 Killed in Aleppo as UN Meets over Syria," ABC News, September 25, 2016. http://abcnews.go.com.

23. Quoted in Nafiseh Kohnavard, "Mosul: Smuggled Diary Reveals Life of Fear Under IS," BBC, September 22, 2016. www .bbc.com/news/world-middle-east-37411167.
24. Quoted in Pamela Engel, "'Unbearable': What Life Is Like Under ISIS in Libya," Business Insider, June 5, 2016. www.busi nessinsider.com.
25. Quoted in Patrick Cockburn, "Life Under ISIS: Eighty Lashes for Cutting His Cousin's Hair," *Newsweek*, May 1, 2016. www.newsweek.com.
26. Quoted in Julia Felsenthal, "Nadia Murad Is Taking On ISIS with the Help of Amal Clooney," *Vogue*, September 26, 2016. www.vogue.com.
27. Quoted in Ashley Gilbertson, "The Child Migrants of Africa," *New York Times*, June 20, 2016. www.nytimes.com.

Chapter 3: The Harsh Reality of Refugee Life

28. Quoted in UN News Centre, "Senior UN Officials Seek Accountability for Human Trafficking Crimes in Forced Migration," September 23, 2016. www.un.org.
29. Quoted in Sally Nyakanyanga, "Pregnant and Homeless: South Sudan's Women Refugees," IRIN, September 30, 2016. www.irinnews.org.
30. Quoted in Paola Brambilla, "Iraq: A Tale of Two Women," Jesuit Refugee Service, February 3, 2016. http://jrsusa.org.
31. Quoted in United Nations High Commissioner for Refugees, "Refugees Fleeing South Sudan Pass One Million Mark," September 16, 2016. www.unhcr.org.
32. Quoted in Nick Squires, "Ninety Per Cent of Migrants and Refugees Crossing Sahara in Hope of Reaching Europe Have Witnessed Death, Torture and Beatings," *Telegraph* (London), September 13, 2016. www.telegraph.co.uk.
33. Quoted in Kareem Shaheen, "Dozens of Syrians Forced into Sexual Slavery in Derelict Lebanese House," *Guardian* (Manchester), April 30, 2016. www.theguardian.com.
34. Quoted in Rachel Middleton, "Turkish Border Police Shooting Refugees Dead as They Flee Syria," *International Business Times*, March 31, 2016. www.ibtimes.co.uk.

35. Quoted in Kingsley, *The New Odyssey*, p. 69.

36. Quoted in Maggie Hyde, "At Least 162 Bodies Recovered After Boat Carrying Hundreds of Refugees Sinks," *Independent* (London), September 23, 2016. www.independent.co.uk.

37. Quoted in Paul Farrell et al., "The Nauru Files: Cache of 2,000 Leaked Reports Reveal Scale of Abuse of Children in Australian Offshore Detention," *Guardian* (Manchester), August 10, 2016. www.theguardian.com.

38. Quoted in Catherine Wachiaya, "From Camp to Campus," United Nations High Commissioner for Refugees, August 12, 2015. www.unhcr.org.

39. Quoted in Gilbertson, "The Child Migrants of Africa."

40. Quoted in *Guardian* (Manchester), "Pope Francis Hailed as Savior by Syrian Refugees Taken In by Vatican," April 17, 2016. www.theguardian.com.

41. Quoted in Zoe Conway and Edward Lawrence, "BBC Helps Bring Afghan Brothers Together," BBC, July 12, 2016. www.bbc.com.

Chapter 4: Beginning Anew

42. Quoted in Hassan Khalifeh, "Syrian Refugees Struggling to Start New Lives," *Dearborn (MI) Arab American News*, July 7, 2016. www.arabamericannews.com.

43. United Nations High Commissioner for Refugees, "Protecting Refugees: Questions and Answers," February 1, 2002. http://www.unhcr.org/en-us/publications/brochures/3b779dfe2/protecting-refugees-questions-answers.html.

44. Quoted in Karolina Tagaris, "Syrian Refugee's Wait for Asylum in Greece Is 'like Death,'" Business Insider, September 23, 2016. www.businessinsider.com.

45. Quoted in Josie Le Blond, "Seeking Refuge from Violence in Afghanistan, Iraq and Syria, They Spent the Summer Months Learning German, Which May Hold the Key to a New Life in Berlin, Germany," United Nations High Commissioner for Refugees, September 15, 2016. www.unhcr.org.

46. Quoted in Chris Parr, "Interview with Melissa Fleming, Spokesperson for the UNHCR," *Times Higher Education*, September 14, 2016. www.timeshighereducation.com.

47. Quoted in Andrea Thomas, "New School Year Brings Test for Integrating Refugees in Germany," *Wall Street Journal*, August 9, 2016. www.wsj.com.

48. Quoted in Malcolm Brabant, "Greece Sends Stranded Refugee Children to School, Stoking Anti-migrant Resistance," *PBS NewsHour*, October 11, 2016. www.pbs.org.

49. Quoted in Stuart Thomson, "Pathologist 'Lucky' to Find Work as Lab Tech in Edmonton After Escape from Syrian Nightmare," *Edmonton Journal*, October 13, 2016. http://edmontonjournal.com.

50. Mark Zuckerberg with Priscilla Chan, Facebook, February 26, 2016. www.facebook.com.

51. David Bier, "Why Refugees Find Jobs Faster in the U.S. than Germany," *Cato at Liberty* (blog), Cato Institute, October 6, 2016. www.cato.org.

52. Quoted in Mike Sackley, "Arizona Refugees Finding Jobs Through Help of Local Organizations," KTAR News, October 5, 2016. http://ktar.com.

53. Quoted in Enjoli Francis and Nick Capote, "'Land of Chances': From Jordan to the US, Syrian Refugees Overcome Obstacles to Start New Life," ABC News, September 20, 2016. http://abcnews.go.com.

54. Quoted in Helena Smith and Patrick Kingsley, "Far-Right Group Attacks Refugee Camp on Greek Island of Chios," *Guardian* (Manchester), November 18, 2016. www.theguardian.com.

55. Quoted in CBS News, "Militia Members Arrested in Alleged Plot Targeting Muslims," October 15, 2016. www.cbsnews.com.

56. Quoted in UNICEF, "Uprooted: The Growing Crisis for Refugee and Migrant Children," September 2016. www.unicef.org.uk.

57. Quoted in Carl Prine, "Syrian Refugees Battle Stereotypes in Fight to Fit in to Western Pennsylvania," *TribLive.com*, October 15, 2016. http://triblive.com.

58. Quoted in Prine, "Syrian Refugees Battle Stereotypes in Fight to Fit In to Western Pennsylvania."

Chapter 5: Dealing with Refugees

59. Quoted in White House, "Remarks by President Obama at Leaders Summit on Refugees," September 20, 2016. www.whitehouse.gov.

60. Quoted in Howard LaFranchi, "UN Makes Big Push to Help Refugees, but Political Tides Have Shifted," *Christian Science Monitor*, September 20, 2016. www.csmonitor.com.

61. Quoted in Amnesty International, "Just 10 of the World's 193 Countries Host More than Half Its Refugees," October 4, 2016. www.amnesty.org.

62. Quoted in Business Insider, "There's a Very Practical Reason Why Germany Is Taking In So Many Refugees," September 10, 2015. www.businessinsider.com.

63. Quoted in Omaira Gill, "Refugee Welcome Begins to Wear Thin in Greece," Deutsche Welle, April 28, 2016. www.dw.com.

64. Quoted in Adam Nossiter, "France Clears 'Jungle' Camp at Calais, Dispersing Thousands of Migrants," *New York Times*, October 24, 2016. www.nytimes.com.

65. Quoted in Philip Oltermann, "Mob Chanting at Bus of Refugees in Germany Shames Politicians," *Guardian* (Manchester), February 19, 2016. www.theguardian.com.

66. Quoted in Pamela Falk, "A Homeless World," *Time*, October 7, 2016, p. 19.

67. Quoted in Alistair Scrutton and Philip Pullella, "Pope Francis Praises Secular Sweden over Asylum Seekers," Reuters, November 1, 2016. www.reuters.com.

68. Quoted in Eunice Ohanusi, "Uganda Farming Classes Transform Refugees into Entrepreneurs," United Nations High Commissioner for Refugees, October 28, 2016. www.unhcr.org.

69. Quoted in Jesuit Refugee Service, "Given the Opportunity We Can Really Do Great Things," June 22, 2016. http://jrsusa.org.

70. Gulwali Passarlay, "At 13 I Found Sanctuary in Britain, Now We're Failing Refugee Children," *Guardian* (Manchester), October 26, 2015. www.theguardian.com.

71. Quoted in Dan Rascon, "Inside the Story: Utah Family In-spired to Start Foundation After Fostering Refugee Teen," KUTV, September 23, 2016. http://kutv.com.

72. Quoted in Rory Linnane, "Refugees Find 'Place to Call Home' in Appleton," *Appleton (WI) Post-Crescent*, November 2, 2016. www.postcrescent.com.

73. Quoted in United Nations High Commissioner for Refugees, "UNHCR Welcomes 'Unprecedented Force and Resonance' of New York Declaration," September 19, 2016. www.unhcr .org.

How to Get Involved

By getting involved, you can make a difference. Organizations that work with groups or issues often need volunteers for a variety of tasks ranging from letter writing to organizing events. Some organizations also sponsor internships for youth.

Catholic Relief Services

228 W. Lexington St.
Baltimore, MD 21201
www.crs.org

This Roman Catholic Agency helps refugees around the world, including those who move to the United States. The agency houses refugees when they flee their homelands to nearby nations and tries to help them move to a final destination to live.

International Rescue Committee

122 E. Forty-Second St.
New York, NY 10168
www.rescue.org

This group works in the United States and other countries to help refugees. It provides housing, food, and medical care. It also offers emergency aid and long-term assistance to refugees and those displaced by war, persecution, or natural disaster.

Islamic Relief USA

PO Box 22250
Alexandria, VA 22304
http://irusa.org

This group works in the United States and other countries to help Muslims, including refugees, make new lives for themselves after they leave their homelands. It provides relief services such as food and medical care as well as educational opportunities.

Jesuit Refugee Service

1016 Sixteenth St. NW, Suite 500
Washington, DC 20036
www.jrsusa.org

This Roman Catholic relief agency helps refugees move to the United States and begin new lives there. It provides housing and aid to refugees and helps them find work so they can support themselves.

Lutheran Immigration and Refugee Service

700 Light St.
Baltimore, MD 21230
http://lirs.org

This Lutheran agency has several ways people can support immigrants and refugees who come to the United States. The organization helps newcomers find housing and jobs, learn English, and otherwise adapt to their new lives.

United Nations High Commissioner for Refugees

Geneva, Switzerland
Case Postale 2500
CH-1211 Genève 2 Dépôt
www.unhcr.org

This UN agency is responsible for helping refugees worldwide. It provides immediate help to people fleeing their homelands, including food, housing, and medical care. It also works to resettle them for the long term.

US Committee for Refugees and Immigrants

2231 Crystal Dr., Suite 350
Arlington, VA 22202
http://refugees.org

This private organization operates offices across the United States to help refugees become accustomed to life there. Founded in 1911 in New York, it provides a variety of services to immigrants and refugees in the nation.

World Vision

PO Box 9716
Federal Way, WA 98063
www.worldvision.org

This Christian group provides humanitarian relief to refugees and other people in need of help around the world. Founded in 1950 to meet the needs of California missionaries, today it is active in ninety nations.

For Further Research

Books

Patrick Kingsley, *The New Odyssey: The Story of Europe's Refugee Crisis*. London: Guardian Faber, 2016.

Gulwali Passarlay, *The Lightless Sky: An Afghan Refugee Boy's Journey of Escape to a New Life in Britain*. London: Atlantic, 2015.

Internet Sources

British Broadcasting Corporation, "Europe Migrant Crisis." www.bbc.com/news/topics/23672ac3-fcad-42c7-a557-23a954eb0e7b/europe-migrant-crisis.

Ian Bremmer, "These 5 Different Camps Tell the Story of the Global Refugee Crisis," *Time*, October 27, 2016. http://time.com/4547918/refugee-camps-calais-zaatari-dadaab-nakivale-mae-la.

Cable News Network, "Seeking Refuge: Migration Crisis." www.cnn.com/specials/world/migration-crisis.

Jodi Kantor and Catrin Einhorn, "Refugees Encounter a Foreign Word: Welcome," *New York Times*, July 1, 2016. www.nytimes.com/2016/07/01/world/americas/canada-syrian-refugees.html.

Nick Evershed et al., "The Lives of Asylum Seekers in Detention Detailed in a Unique Database," *Guardian* (Manchester), August 10, 2016. www.theguardian.com/australia-news/ng-interactive/2016/aug/10/the-nauru-files-the-lives-of-asylum-seekers-in-detention-detailed-in-a-unique-database-interactive.

Brita Ohm, "Berlin Attack on the Media Stereotypes About Refugees." Deutsche-Welle.com, December 23, 2016. www.dw.com/en/berlin-attack-and-the-media-stereotypes-about-refugees/a-36888614.

Websites

International Organization for Migration (www.iom.int). The media center for this group has information and stories about refugees and migrants as they move around the world and try to find new places to live.

Patrick Kingsley, *Guardian* (www.theguardian.com/profile/patrick-kingsley). This reporter for the *Guardian* newspaper was named foreign affairs journalist of the year at the 2015 British Journalism Awards. He has written a book and numerous articles about the European refugee crisis. This site features his extensive reporting.

United Nations High Commissioner for Refugees (www.unhcr.org). The UN agency for refugees compiles extensive information, stories, and facts about refugees.

Index

Picture Credits

About the Author

Michael V. Uschan has written 101 books, including *Life of an American Soldier in Iraq*, for which he won the 2005 Council for Wisconsin Writers Juvenile Nonfiction Award. It was the second time he won the award. Uschan began his career as a writer and editor with United Press International, a wire service that provided stories to newspapers, radio, and television. He and his wife, Barbara, reside in the Milwaukee suburb of Franklin, Wisconsin.